STARK LIBRARY   May 2021

S0-ABR-165

For Talie
and Elias, two
little gems
— K. D.

A Rainbow of Rocks

WRITTEN BY Kate DePalma

Barefoot Books
Step inside a story

claystone

Claystone is
crumbly and crushable!

Ruby is
near unbreakable.

ruby

Copper gives sunstone its fiery glow.

Sunstone

Iron makes citrine rusty, though!

Citrine

Pyrite cubes reflect the light.

Pyrite

Calcite is glassy — edged with white.

calcite

emerald

This emerald glistens deepest green.

jade

That jade is the palest shade I've seen!

sapphire

Sapphire lets the sun shine through.

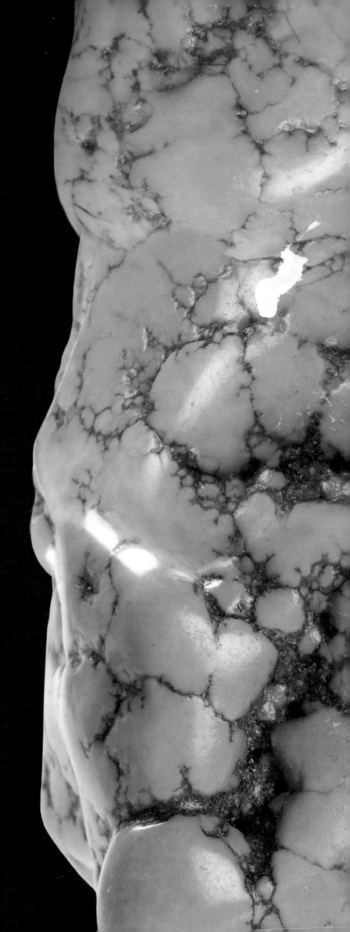

turquoise

Light reflects off turquoise blue.

Fluorite crystals look like squares.

fluorite

Amethyst

points up everywhere!

amethyst

is black
and smooth
as glass.

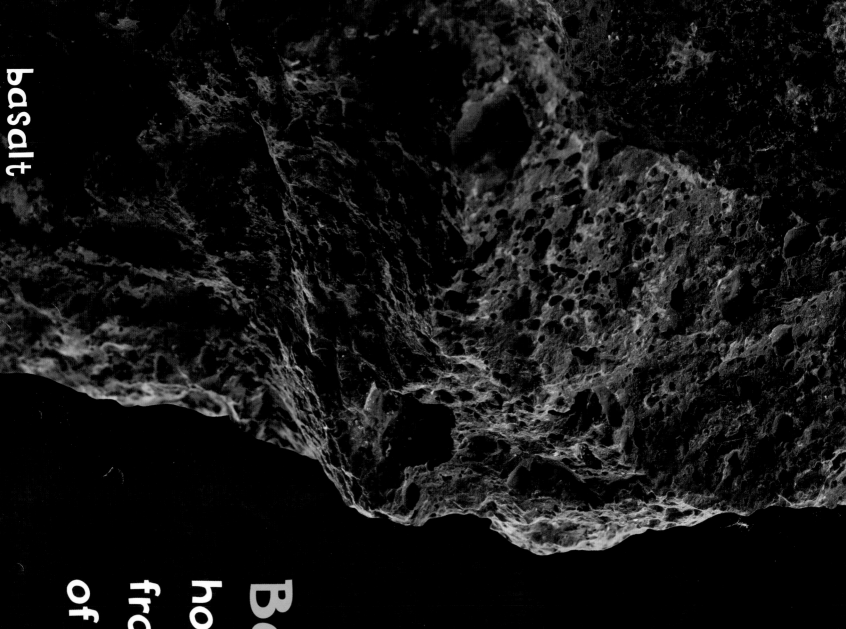

basalt

Basalt's
holes come
from bubbles
of gas.

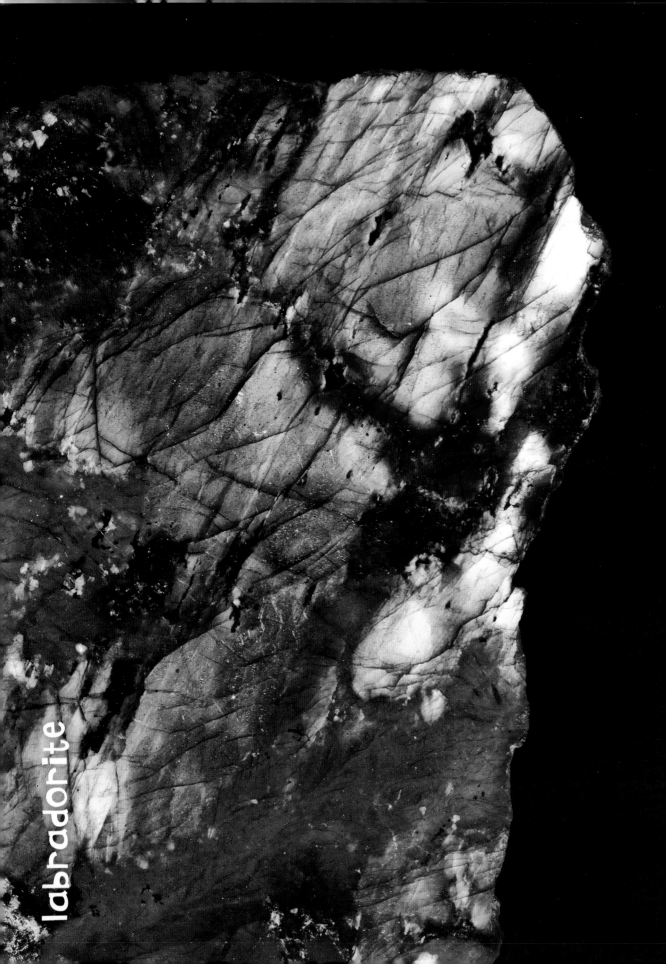

labradorite

labradorite seems to glow.

Bornite shines like a rainbow.

bornite

Rocks in every shape and hue.

Each one's different, just like you!

Questions to ask about

Are rocks alive?

No. Plants, animals and people are living, or **organic** — rocks are not! Rocks are not living, or **non-organic.**

What are minerals?

Minerals are solids that are created naturally in the earth. The tiny building blocks (atoms) that make minerals form in special repeating patterns. A **rock** is a clump of one or more minerals.

How are rocks formed?

All rocks come from other rocks! One type of rock is formed when lava (hot melted rock) spews out of a volcano and hardens as it cools. A second type of rock is formed when sand and clay (tiny broken pieces of other rocks) are carried by wind and water to the ocean, where they stick together. And a third type of rock is created when heat and pressure change an existing rock.

Did you know?

The outer layer of our planet Earth is made of rocks!

How hard are they?

Scientists give the **hardness** of rocks and minerals a number from 1 to 10 on a scale called the Mohs scale, where 10 is the hardest mineral and 1 is the softest. **Ruby** is one of the hardest minerals at a 9 on the Mohs scale, but **claystone** is closer to 2.5, making it much softer.

claystone

ruby

rocks and minerals

Sunstone

What are they made of?

Small amounts of other materials called **impurities** can change the way rocks and minerals look. **Sunstone** gets its fiery, sparkly appearance from tiny amounts of the metal copper inside it. **Citrine** contains the metal iron, which often gives a rusty hue.

citrine

Pyrite

Are they shiny or dull?

Lustre is the word scientists use to describe the way rocks and minerals look when light hits them. **Pyrite** is very shiny and looks like metal — that's why it is sometimes called fool's gold! But **calcite** looks more like cloudy glass. Rocks can also look earthy, silky or even greasy!

calcite

More questions to ask

jade

How deep or pale is the shade?

Rocks and minerals come in a rainbow of **hues**, some very deep and dark and others very pale and light. The most valuable **emeralds** are known for being a deep, dark green. The mineral **jade** can range from dark green to a pale, almost white hue.

emerald

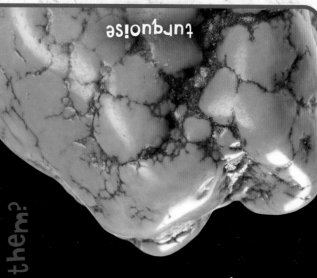

turquoise

Does light shine through them?

Scientists use the word **transparency** to describe how light shines through rocks and minerals. A little bit of light can pass through **sapphire**, so it is called translucent. But light cannot pass through **turquoise**, so it is called opaque.

sapphire

what do they feel like?

You can feel the **texture** of rocks and minerals by touching them. **Obsidian** feels smooth like glass. When **basalt** is formed, sometimes air bubbles get trapped inside and create holes, which can make it feel bumpy. Both are created when lava from a volcano cools down.

obsidian

basalt

what shape are they?

Rocks and minerals form in many different **shapes**. **Fluorite** crystals are shaped like cubes. Most **amethyst** is made of clumps of six-sided crystals that end in six-sided pyramids.

fluorite

amethyst

labradorite

bornite

What happens as light moves across them?

Some rocks and minerals shine differently as light moves across them. The word **iridescence** comes from the Greek word for rainbow. An iridescent mineral like **bornite** changes hue as light moves across it. When light hits **labradorite** it looks so unique that it has its own tongue-twisting name: labradorescence!

The publisher would like to thank geology specialist Daniel P. Babin for his expert review of this book.

Barefoot Books
2067 Massachusetts Ave
Cambridge, MA 02140

Barefoot Books
29/30 Fitzroy Square
London, W1T 6LQ

Text copyright © 2020 by Kate DePalma
The moral rights of Kate DePalma
have been asserted

First published in United States of America
by Barefoot Books, Inc and in Great Britain
by Barefoot Books, Ltd in 2020
All rights reserved

Graphic design by Elizabeth Kaleko
and Sarah Soldano, Barefoot Books
Reproduction by Bright Arts, Hong Kong
Printed in China on 100% acid-free paper
This book was typeset in Century Gothic,
Hoagie and Johann

Photographs copyright ©:
asife/Shutterstock.com (amethyst), Asya Babushkina/Shutterstock.com (turquoise),
Cagla Acikgoz/Shutterstock.com (fluorite), Coldmoon Photoproject/Shutterstock.com
(citrine), Eky Studio/Shutterstock.com (black texture), Fokin Oleg/Shutterstock.com
(claystone), hjochen/Shutterstock.com (bornite), Imfoto/Shutterstock.com (sunstone),
kongsky/Shutterstock.com (jade), Moha El-Jaw/Shutterstock.com (calcite),
olpo/Shutterstock.com (labradorite), photo-world/Shutterstock.com (emerald),
Potapov Alexander/Shutterstock.com (ruby, sapphire), Suto Norbert Zsolt/Shutterstock.com
(pyrite), TuktaBaby/Shutterstock.com (basalt), Victorstock/Shutterstock.com
(white texture), vvoe/Shutterstock.com (obsidian)

Hardback ISBN 978-1-78285-986-4 | Paperback ISBN 978-1-78285-992-5
E-book ISBN 978-1-64686-046-3

British Cataloging-in-Publication Data: a catalogue record
for this book is available from the British Library

Library of Congress Cataloging-in-Publication Data is available upon request

3 5 7 9 8 6 4 2

Barefoot Books
Step inside a story

At Barefoot Books, we celebrate art and story that opens the hearts and minds of children from all walks of life, focusing on themes that encourage independence of spirit, enthusiasm for learning and respect for the world's diversity. The welfare of our children is dependent on the welfare of the planet, so we source paper from sustainably managed forests and constantly strive to reduce our environmental impact. Playful, beautiful and created to last a lifetime, our products combine the best of the present with the best of the past to educate our children as the caretakers of tomorrow.

www.barefootbooks.com

3133305101919733